Steven Mackey

Cairn

for Electric Guitar and Effects Loop

Playing Score

Archive Edition

HENDON MUSIC

BOOSEY & HAWKES

AN IMAGEM COMPANY

DISTRIBUTED BY

HAL•LEONARD®
CORPORATION
7777 W. BLUEMOUND RD. P.O. BOX 13819 MILWAUKEE, WI 53213

www.boosey.com
www.halleonard.com

Premiered June 21, 1994, Roulette, New York,
Steven Mackey on Guitar

Duration: 5 minutes

Equipment :

Electric Guitar

Effects processing - - distortion, delay, chorus, EQ.

Sampler/Looping Echo device (ie. Lexicon Jam-Man)

Notation : ⨍ = quarter tone sharp;   ɸ = quarter tone flat

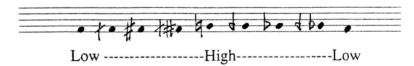

Low -------------------High------------------Low

Cairn

Steven Mackey (1994)

♩ = 66 *rubato but, with a lilt,*
       a cross between Webern and Piazzola
Sound: clean, classic jazz, a little delay ca. mm.132

* forcefully dampen all but string IV and create
percussive attack by slapping right hand down on strings.
Thumb can dampen VI and V, index, middle and ring can
dampen III, II, and I respectively.

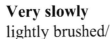

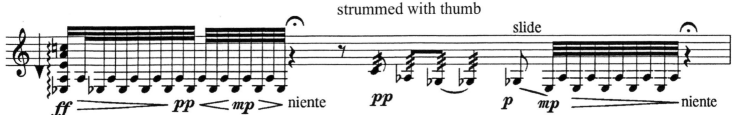

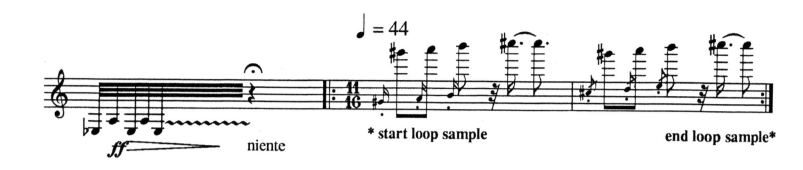

♩ = 44

* start loop sample

end loop sample*

ff niente

improvised solo over sampler ostinato (30-90 sec.)

*

sampler:

* Whatever else happens in the solo, the line G# - F# - E #
should occur, either embeded throughout the course of the solo
or all at once as the final phrase of the solo. At any rate,
the E# should be the last tone of the solo before proceeding.

end of solo

sampler:

sampler: played live

Rit.   a tempo   hold back   a tempo,
                                        slide

p   *p*

* forcefully dampen all but string IV and create
percussive attack by slapping right hand down on strings.
Thumb can dampen VI and V, index, middle and ring can
dampen III, II, and I respectively.

still rubato but moving forward

Rit.

bend

mf

mp

broaden slightly

a tempo

molto Rit.

r.h. nat. harm.

Rit.

slower

VI

VI VI

IV

n. < *p*   n. < *p*

let A ring throughout

* art. harm. l.h. stops C, r.h. touches node 8ve above
(w/index fing.) and plucks.